Contents

INTRODUCTION

The rice diet is a low-calorie, low-sodium diet created by Dr. Walter Kempner in 1939. While working as a professor at the Duke University in Durham, North Carolina, Dr. Kempner created a dietary approach to help his patients lower blood pressure, improve kidney function, and keep a check on obesity.

The reason this diet works for treating people with hypertension or obesity lies in the foods allowed for consumption. It includes foods high in complex carbs, limited dairy, and foods low in sodium.

Complex carbs take longer to get digested, thereby reducing hunger.

Low-sodium intake prevents the body from storing excess water weight and reduces the pressure on the kidneys.

A low-calorie diet (800 calories per day) is allowed initially, which is then increased up to 1200 calories per day.

In a nutshell, low-calorie, low-sodium, and high-fiber foods are the reasons behind the success of the rice diet. Now, let's check out what foods you should consume and what to avoid and including recipes to make

RICE DIET

The rice diet is a low-calorie, low-sodium diet created by Dr. Walter Kempner in 1939. While working as a professor at the Duke University in Durham, North Carolina, Dr. Kempner created a dietary approach to help his patients lower blood pressure, improve kidney function, and keep a check on obesity.

The reason this diet works for treating people with hypertension or obesity lies in the foods allowed for consumption. It includes foods high in complex carbs, limited dairy, and foods low in sodium.

Complex carbs take longer to get digested, thereby reducing hunger.

Low-sodium intake prevents the body from storing excess water weight and reduces the pressure on the kidneys.

A low-calorie diet (800 calories per day) is allowed initially, which is then increased up to 1200 calories per day.

In a nutshell, low-calorie, low-sodium, and high-fiber foods are the reasons behind the success of the rice diet.

RICE DIET FOOD LISTS

To Consume

The rice diet is quite restrictive. On this diet, you will be consuming:

- Fresh fruits
- Vegetables
- Low-salt beans
- Whole grains
- Lean protein
- Non-fat dairy

To Avoid

- Junk food
- Soda
- Bottled fruit juices

- Candies

- Milk chocolate

- Frozen food

- Deep-fried food

- Ready-to-eat foods

- Refined flour, refined sugar, and trans fat foods

You will need to dump all the junk food and adopt better eating and lifestyle choices.

WHITE RICE OR BROWN RICE?

It depends. If you like having white rice, go for it! And if you choose to consume brown rice, you can do it. Brown rice is considered healthier as it contains more dietary fiber. But you may compensate for that by adding extra veggies to your bowl of white rice.

Taste-wise, white rice is certainly more palatable. But you might like the chewy texture of brown rice (takes longer to cook and needs to be soaked for at least 20 minutes).

RICE DIET PLAN

Phase 1 – 800 calories

Day 1

Breakfast (8:00 a.m.) 1 medium bowl of oatmeal with banana and chia seeds

Lunch (12:00 p.m.) Rice + stir-fried veggies + baked fish

Snack (3:30 p.m.) 300 mL freshly pressed fruit juice

Dinner (6:30 p.m.) Grilled chicken and mushroom rice

Phase 2 – 1000 calories

Breakfast (8:00 a.m.) 1 toast + ½ avocado + ½ small bowl of homemade ricotta cheese + 1 cup green tea

Lunch (12:00 p.m.) Rice + stir-fried veggies + grilled chicken

Snack (3:30 p.m.) 1 cup of mixed fruits

Dinner (6:30 p.m.) Vegetable and fish sushi

Phase 3 – 1200 calories

Breakfast (8:00 a.m.) A medium bowl of vegetable quinoa + 1 cup green tea

Lunch (12:00 p.m.) Rice + stir-fried veggies + baked fish or fish curry

Snack (3:30 p.m.) 1 cup buttermilk + 10 in-shell pistachios

Dinner (6:30 p.m.) Low-fat chicken and mushroom risotto

It is a tough diet to follow. So, it's best to follow it for not more than two weeks. The rice diet has undergone modification as the nutritional requirements, food habits, and scientific view on food and nutrition have changed.

It is a tough diet to follow. So, it's best to follow it for not more than two weeks. The rice diet has undergone modification as the nutritional requirements, food habits, and scientific view on food and nutrition have changed.

You must take care of your sleep pattern. Sleep deprivation is one of the causes of toxin build-up in the body. The harmful free oxygen radicals alter your DNA and cause numerous health problems, including obesity, diabetes, and heart disease.

Meditate for at least five minutes a day: Increase the duration as you become more comfortable.

Avoid alcohol: You may consume 30 mL of wine once a week.

Workout regularly: You will start seeing a change in your mood and energy levels from the very first day you exercise.

Drink at least two liters of water per day: You may add citrus fruits, mint leaves, ginger, and cucumber to make your bottle of water more palatable.

Eat at regular intervals: Going on a hunger strike will only weaken your bones, muscles, and brain function.

It is clear that, along with diet, you must follow a healthy lifestyle to keep yourself fit and happy. But, for that, you can follow a diet that's not so restrictive.

WHO SHOULD FOLLOW THE RICE DIET?

You may follow this diet if:

- You have high blood pressure.
- You have diabetes.
- You have heart disease.
- You suffer from chronic renal failure.
- You have high cholesterol.
- You are gluten sensitive.

BENEFITS OF THE RICE DIET

- May help reduce body fat.

- May help reduce cholesterol levels.

- May help lower blood pressure.

- May improve heart health.

- May protect from diabetes type II.

SIDE EFFECTS OF THE RICE DIET

- May cause nutritional deficiencies.

- You may get bored of the diet and feel starved.

- You may feel irritated.

- May cause nausea.

- May lead to weakness.

The rice diet is an effective diet. But, it is also a very, very restrictive diet. Unless you have a health condition that requires you to be on this diet, and no other diet will work, you may follow the rice diet. If you are looking for a weight loss diet, the rice diet might not be the ultimate diet plan. Talk to your doctor today and get expert opinion before you decide to be on this diet.

RICE DIET COOKBOOK

There are many foods thatfit into the rice diet plan. "The Rice Diet Cookbook" offers up several mouthwatering recipes, like French toast sticks, two-bean chili, macaroni and cheese, and, of course, rice recipes like brown rice salad.

FRENCH TOAST

This recipe can even be made ahead of time and reheated for busy mornings.

Ingredients

- 1 cup non-dairy milk
- 1/2 cup orange juice
- 2 tbsp. flour

- 1 tbsp. sugar

- 1 tbsp. nutritional yeast

- 1/2 tsp. cinnamon

- 1/4 tsp. nutmeg

- 6-8 slices of bread

Directions

- Mix all ingredients except the bread together. Dip bread in the mixture and heat on a skillet.

SAVORY RICE

The rice diet wouldn't be complete without rice, right? This recipe can be cooked and used for many servings throughout the week.

Ingredients

- 1 cup brown rice, cooked

- 4 tbsp. onions, chopped

- 2 tbsp. parsley, chopped

- 2 cloves of garlic, minced

- 1 tsp. paprika

Directions

- Heat the garlic and onion with the rice, then sprinkle with the parsley and paprika while still warm.

CHICKEN AND RICE

Ingredients

- 1 tbsp olive oil

- 6-8 chicken thighs can use breasts but they dry out more easily

- 1 tsp kosher salt plus more to taste

- 1 tsp ground black pepper plus more to taste

- 1 medium onion chopped

- 3 cloves garlic minced

- 15 cremini mushrooms quartered

- 2 1/2 cups brown rice can use white rice

- 1/2 cup pearl barley optional - if not
  using, just use additional rice

- 5 cups chicken broth

Instructions

- Heat olive oil over medium-high heat in a
  deep skillet that also has a lid. Generously
  coat the chicken with kosher salt and
  ground black pepper. Cook the chicken
  until it is well browned on each side. Once
  browned, remove the chicken and place
  aside on a plate, reserving the pan
  drippings.

- In the same pan, add the onion and cook
  until tender, about 6-8 minutes. Add the
  garlic and cook 1 minute. Add the
  mushrooms, rice and barley and cook an
  additional 5 minutes.

- Add the chicken broth and stir well to combine. Place the chicken on top of the mixture, including any juices from the plate.

- Bring to a simmer, cover and let cook approximately 45-60 minutes or until chicken broth is absorbed and rice and barley is fully cooked, stirring occasionally so as not to allow the rice to stick to the pan.

EASY BROWN RICE

Ingredients

- 2 ½ cups water or broth
- 1 cup brown rice

Directions

- Combine water (or broth) and rice in a medium saucepan. Bring to a boil. Reduce heat to low, cover and simmer until tender and most of the liquid has been absorbed, 40 to 50 minutes. Let stand 5 minutes, then fluff with a fork.

HEALTHY FRIED RICE RECIPE

INGREDIENTS

- 1 tablespoon macadamia nut oil OR avocado oil (or other healthy cooking oil), divided
- 3 large eggs
- 5–6 scallions (aka green onions), root and 2 inches of green top removed, chopped (about 1/2 cup)
- 1 large carrot, shredded or julienned (about 1/2 cup)
- 1/2 cup frozen peas
- 2 cups cooked brown rice

- 3 tablespoons organic tamari* or low
  sodium soy sauce
- 1 teaspoon rice vinegar (no sugar added)
- 1 teaspoon toasted sesame oil
- 1/2 teaspoon freshly grated ginger
- sea salt
- fresh cracked black pepper

INSTRUCTIONS

- Heat 1/2 tablespoon oil over medium
  heat.
- In a mixing bowl, whisk the eggs into a
  uniform mixture until well combine and
  season with a small pinch of sea salt and
  fresh black pepper.
- Add the eggs to the pan and scramble.
  Once cooked remove the scrambled eggs
  from the pan to a plate and reserve for
  later.

- Add the remaining 1/2 tablespoon oil to
  the pan over medium heat; add the
  scallions and carrot and sauté 3-4 minutes
  until softened.
- Add the frozen peas to the pan, then add
  the rice, tamari, rice vinegar, toasted
  sesame oil and ginger. Stir well to
  combine, the heat from the pan will
  quickly defrost the peas.
- Turn off the heat and stir in the scrambled
  eggs. Season with a pinch of sea salt if
  needed—it will depend on the sodium
  content of the tamari and other
  ingredients.
- Turn the heat to low and cook another 5
  minutes until the entire dish is warmed
  through.
- Water chestnuts, bean sprouts, edamame
  and just about any other veggie you like

would also be a delicious addition to this dish.

HEALTHY FRIED RICE

Ingredients

- 2 tablespoons toasted sesame oil
- 1 lb boneless skinless chicken breasts cut into 1 inch cubes
- 1 cup onion finely chopped
- 1 tablespoon garlic finely minced
- 1 cup peppers diced finely
- 1 cup carrots finely chopped
- 1 teaspoon ground ginger
- 1/2 teaspoon pepper
- 1/2 cup coconut aminos
- 1/4 teaspoon red pepper flakes optional- omit if you like less spice
- 2 eggs
- 1 cup frozen green peas

- 2 cups cooked rice

Instructions

- In a pan, heat 1 tablespoon toasted sesame oil. Sauté chicken for 15-20 minutes until brown on edges. Remove chicken from the pan and set aside.
- In the same pan, add additional tablespoon of sesame oil. Heat the oil and sauté onions, garlic, peppers, carrots and spices until vegetables start to soften, approximately 5 minutes.
- Stir in cooked rice. Push rice/veggies to the side of the pan
- In a small bowl, whisk together eggs until combined. Add eggs to the pan and scramble on the empty side of the pan. Stir together with rice/veggie mixture and cook for 1-2 minutes until eggs are cooked.

- Add cooked chicken, coconut aminos +
  peas to the pan, stir together until
  combined
- Serve with sesame seeds or chopped
  scallions + enjoy!

20 MINUTE MEAL-PREP CHICKEN, RICE, AND BROCCOLI

Ingredients

For the Rice:

- 2 cups water
- 1 cup jasmine rice
- 3/4 teaspoon salt

For the chicken:

- 4 small-medium boneless skinless chicken
  breasts or thighs about 4 oz each
- 1 teaspoon brown or granulated sugar
- 1/2 teaspoon paprika
- 1/2 teaspoon cumin

- 1/2 teaspoon garlic powder

- Salt and pepper to taste

- 1 tablespoon olive oil

- 2-3 cups broccoli florets

- water for steaming

Instructions

- To Cook the Rice:Bring the water to a boil in a medium saucepan. this Stir in the rice; cover and reduce the heat to low. Simmer for 15 minutes until all of the water is absorbed.

- To Cook the chicken: Rub chicken with brown sugar, paprika, cumin, garlic powder, salt, and pepper. Heat 1-2 tablespoons oil in a large heavy-duty pan or skillet over medium-high heat.

- Add the chicken to pan and cook for 5-6 minutes on the first side without moving, until the undersides develop dark grill

marks. Flip the chicken breasts using a
pair of tongs or a fork and cook the other
side for 5-6 minutes. Turn off heat and
allow chicken breasts to rest in pan for at
least 5 minutes before cutting.

- To steam broccoli: There are two ways to
cook the broccoli. To blanch the broccoli
on the stove-top. Boil water in a large pot.
Add broccoli florets to pot and blanch for
just 1 minute. Remove from the pot. To
steam in the microwave: Place broccoli in
a microwave-safe bowl and add water 3
tablespoons water to the bowl. Cover
with a ceramic plate or plastic wrap.
Microwave on high for 3 minutes.

- To assemble: Cut the chicken into slices or
small bite-size pieces. Use a 1 cup
measuring cup to evenly spoon 1 cup of
rice into each (4 total) Top the rice with
slices chicken and broccoli florets. Cover

and refrigerate for you to 4 days. To
reheat microwave on high for 2 minutes
or until steaming.

EASY FRIED RICE

Ingredients

- 80 g chicken, breast alternatively 1/2 cup leftover shredded chicken meat
- 1 egg
- 1 clove garlic crushed
- ½ cup peas, fresh or frozen
- ½ cup capsicum finely diced
- 1 onion, spring thinly sliced
- 1 tbsp soy sauce salt-reduced, gluten free if required
- 1 tsp oil, canola
- 1 cup rice, brown cooked, or instant microwave variety

Instructions

- Poach chicken breast in saucepan of boiling water for 10 mins. Drain and dice the cooked chicken. If using pre-cooked chicken, skip this step.
- Cook the rice as per packet instructions. If using instant microwave rice, heat the rice as per packet instructions.
- Heat oil in fry pan on medium heat. Whisk egg in a bowl and then pour into fry pan—do not mix once added to pan, you want it to be an omelette. Cook for 2-3 mins before flipping. Cook for another minute on this side, then remove from the pan. Cut omelette into thin slices.
- Add the crushed garlic, peas and capsicum to the pan. Cook for 2 mins.
- Add the cooked chicken, egg, rice and soy sauce. Cook for another minute.

- Serve onto a plate and sprinkle with sliced spring onion.

LOW-CARB CAULIFLOWER RICE

Ingredients

- 1½ lbs cauliflower
- ½ tsp salt
- ½ tsp turmeric (optional)
- 3 oz. butter or coconut oil

Instructions

- Using a grater or grater attachment on a food processor, shred the entire cauliflower head.
- Melt butter or coconut oil in a skillet. Add the cauliflower and cook over medium heat for 5-10 minutes or until the riced cauliflower has softened a bit.

- Add salt and the optional turmeric while frying.

LOW-CARB RICE WITH HONEY RECIPE

INGREDIENTS:

- 1 cup organic sushi rice
- 1 ½ cups water
- Pinch of Himalayan pink salt
- 2 tbsp. grass-fed butter
- 1 tsp. raw honey
- 3 tbsp. coconut oil

INSTRUCTIONS:

- Bring water to a boil.
- Rinse rice well in cold water and drain.
- Add rice and coconut oil, reduce heat to low, cover, and cook for 20 minutes.
- Remove rice from heat and immediately transfer it to the fridge. Let rice cool in the

fridge for 1 hour, or longer. You can portion out the rice before putting it in the fridge so that it cools more quickly. (Think chunks shaped like your thumb, like you'd use for nigiri sushi)

- When rice is cool, set oven to warm.
- Remove rice from fridge and put in oven until warm.
- Drizzle butter, raw honey, and salt.
- Enjoy.

HOW TO MAKE PERFECTLY COOKED BROWN RICE

Ingredients

- 2 1/4 cup filtered water
- 1 cup dry brown rice
- 1/2 teaspoon kosher salt

Instructions

- Add water and salt in a small pot (I used a 2.5 quart pot) and bring to a boil. Stir in ric and bring back up to a boil.

- Turn the heat to low so that you have a gentle simmer and pop on the lid. Set your timer for 30 minutes.

- After 30 minutes, begin to check the rice. Once the water has absorbed, shut off the heat and let the pot sit on the stove (with the lid on!) for 15 minutes.

- Remove the lid and stir you light fluffy rice. Enjoy!

GREEK LEMON RICE RECIPE

INGREDIENTS

- 2 cups long grain rice (uncooked)

- Early Harvest Greek extra virgin olive oil

- 1 medium yellow onion, chopped (just over 1 cup chopped onions)

- 1 garlic clove, minced

- 1/2 cup orzo pasta

- 2 lemons, juice of (PLUS zest of 1 lemon)

- 2 cups low sodium broth (chicken or vegetable broth will work)

- Pinch salt

- Large handful chopped fresh parsley

- 1 tsp dill weed (dry dill)

INSTRUCTIONS

- Wash rice well and then soak it for about 15 to 20 minutes in plenty of cold water (enough to cover the rice by 1 inch). You should be able to easily break a grain of rice by simply placing it between your thumb and index finger. Drain well.

- Heat about 3 tbsp extra virgin olive oil in a large sauce pan with a lid (like this one) until oil is shimmering but not smoking. Add onions and cook for about 3 to 4 minutes until translucent. Add garlic and orzo pasta. Toss around for a bit until the orzo has gained some color then stir in the rice. Toss to coat.

- Now add lemon juice and broth. Bring liquid to a rolling boil (it should reduce a little), then turn heat to low. Cover and let cook for about 20 minutes or until rice is done (liquid should be fully absorbed and rice should be tender but not sticky.)
- Remove rice from heat. For best results, leave it covered and do not disturb rice for about 10 minutes or so.
- Uncover and stir in parsley, dill weed and lemon zest. If you like, add a few slices of lemon on top for garnish. Enjoy!

NOTES

- Cook's tip #1: Do not skip washing and soaking the rice well, this is important to help get rid of excess starch which causes rice to be sticky (this rice is not meant to be sticky). Soaking the rice here also shortens the cooking time, making sure the interior of the grain actually cooks before the exterior looses its shape.

- Cook's Tip # 2: Once rice is finished, leave it covered and undisturbed in the pot for about 10 minutes before adding the herbs etc. Again, this helps maintain the texture and integrity of the rice.

EASY LOW-CARB CAULIFLOWER FRIED RICE RECIPE

Ingredients

- 2 tablespoons butter, ghee, coconut oil, or olive oil
- 12 ounces riced cauliflower fresh or frozen

- 1/4 cup carrot finely diced (optional)

- 1 ounce green onion (about 2 large or 4 small) sliced, with white and green parts separated

- 2 cloves garlic crushed

- 1 large egg beaten

- 2 tablespoons gluten-free soy sauce or Tamari (more or less to taste)

- 1 teaspoon toasted sesame oil

Instructions

- In a large heavy skillet or wok, melt butter or oil of choice over medium-high heat.

- Add carrots and riced cauliflower. Cook, stirring occasionally, until vegetables begin to soften--about 5 minutes.

- Stir in the white part of the green onions. Cook until vegetables are almost tender-- about 2-3 minutes more. Add the garlic and cook for 1 minute.

- Pour in the egg and stir it together with the vegetables. Cook, stirring the mixture frequently, until the egg is scrambled. This takes about 1-2 minutes.

- Stir in the soy sauce, green part of green onions, and the sesame oil. Taste and adjust seasoning.

RAINBOW RICE AND CHICKEN SALAD

Ingredients

- 1 small gem lettuce
- 8 tablespoons cold pre-cooked brown rice (60g uncooked weight)
- 150g cold cooked chicken, cut into bite-sized pieces
- 2 medium tomatoes, diced
- 5cm piece of cucumber, diced
- 2 spring onions, finely chopped
- 1 small yellow pepper, diced

- 1 ring pineapple canned in natural juice, drained and cut into small pieces

- ½ red apple, diced (use lemon juice to prevent it turning brown)

- 4 dried apricots, finely chopped

- ½ tablespoon sultanas

- 1 tablespoon flaked almonds

For the vinaigrette:

- 1 teaspoon olive oil

- 2 teaspoons white wine vinegar

- Freshly ground black pepper

- 1 tablespoon low-fat Greek yoghurt

Directions

- Arrange the lettuce leaves on serving plates to look like petals.

- Place the rice and chicken in a mixing bowl with the remaining ingredients and stir gently together.

- Make the vinaigrette by mixing the ingredients together. Dress the salad with the vinaigrette and toss lightly. Spoon the salad on to the prepared serving plates on top of the lettuce leaves.

MEDITERRANEAN SPICED RICE WITH BLACK BEANS & CHICKPEAS

Ingredients

- 2 T olive oil
- 6 cloves garlic, minced
- 1 cup uncooked basmati rice
- ¼ tsp salt
- ½ tsp cumin
- 1/2 tsp sumac (optional)
- ½ tsp turmeric
- ½ tsp smoked paprika
- ½ tsp cayenne pepper
- 1 ¾ cups chicken or vegetable stock

- 1 can (30 oz) chickpeas, drained and rinsed
- 1 can(30 oz) black beans, drained and rinsed
- 1 bunch parsley, chopped (set aside a few sprigs unchopped for garnish)
- juice of ½ lemon
- 1 tomato, chopped or cut into thin slices
- 1/2 cup Greek yogurt
- 1 bunch scallions, chopped

Instructions

- Heat the olive oil in a large saucepan over medium heat. Stir in garlic, and cook 1 minute.
- Stir in rice, salt, cumin, sumac (optional), turmeric, paprika and cayenne pepper. Cook and stir 5 minutes, then pour in chicken stock.

- Bring to a boil. Reduce heat to low, cover, and simmer 20 minutes.

- Gently mix chick peas, black beans, parsley, and lemon juice into the cooked rice.

- Cook another 5 minutes on low heat.

- Garnish with whole parsley leaves, tomatoes, a dollop of Greek yogurt and scallions.

CARIBBEAN RICE

Ingredients

- 4 cups vegetable broth

- 1 onion, chopped

- 1-2 cloves garlic, crushed or minced

- 1 (4-ounce) can chopped green chiles

- 3 cups peeled and chopped butternut squash

- 2 teaspoons curry powder

- 1 teaspoon ground coriander

- ½ teaspoon ground cumin

- Freshly ground black pepper

- 1 cup long-grain brown rice

- ½ cup wild rice

- 1 (15-ounce) can kidney beans, drained and rinsed

- 1 cup chopped Swiss chard

- ¾ cup chopped scallions, white and green parts

Instructions

- Put ½ cup of the broth into a large saucepan and add the onion, garlic, and chiles. Cook, stirring occasionally, until the onion softens, about 5 minutes.

- Stir in the squash, curry powder, coriander, cumin, and pepper to taste, and cook for 2 minutes. Add both types of rice and the remaining 3½ cups broth.

Bring to a boil, reduce the heat, cover, and simmer gently until the rice is tender, about 45 minutes.

- Stir in the beans, chard, and scallions and cook until they are heated through and the chard is tender, about 5 minutes. Serve hot.

ZUCCHINI, BLACK BEANS AND RICE SUPPER

Ingredients

- 1 tablespoon canola oil
- 1-1/2 cups fresh zucchini
- 15 ounces canned no-salt-added black beans
- 1 medium tomato
- 1 cup water
- 1 cup instant white rice, uncooked

- 1/4 cup shredded cheddar and Monterey jack cheese blend

Directions

- In a large skillet, heat oil over medium-high heat.
- Slice zucchini lengthwise and chop.
- Add zucchini to skillet and sauté until tender, stirring often.
- Drain and rinse black beans from the can, then add beans to the skillet.
- Chop tomato and add to skillet along with water.
- Increase heat and bring to a boil.
- Add rice; stir well.
- Remove from heat and let stand 7 minutes or until liquid is absorbed.
- Sprinkle each portion with 1 tablespoon cheese blend, if desired.

EASY & HEALTHY FRIED RICE

Ingredients

- 2 tablespoons sesame oil
- 3 cloves garlic, minced
- 2 chicken breasts, diced
- salt, to taste
- pepper, to taste
- 1 cup carrot(120 g), diced
- 1 cup broccoli floret(175 g)
- 2 cups brown rice(400 g), cooked
- ½ cup frozen peas(75 g)
- 3 tablespoons low sodium soy sauce

Direction

- Heat sesame oil in a skillet, and cook garlic until softened.
- Add the chicken, salt, and pepper, and sauté for 5 minutes.
- Add the carrots and broccoli, and sauté until tender.

- Add the rice, soy sauce, and peas, and mix thoroughly.
- Enjoy!

LOW-FAT CHICKEN FRIED RICE

Ingredients

- Low-fat cooking spray
- 3 eggs plus 2 egg whites lightly beaten
- ground black pepper
- 2 cups long-grain rice cooked and chilled
- 7 water chestnuts sliced
- 1 tablespoon anchovy paste
- 1 tablespoon light soy sauce or more depending on taste
- 1 tablespoon light-dark soy sauce
- 2 spring onions trimmed and sliced into rounds
- 1 cup leftover or cooked chicken or whatever meat you want to use

Instructions

- Heat a non-stick wok until hot and coat with cooking spray.
- Pour in the eggs and scramble, scraping the bits that stick to the wok. Once cooked, remove from the wok and set aside.
- Add a bit more cooking spray to the wok. Add spring onions and anchovy paste and heat through.
- Add the rice, scraping the bottom of the wok and tossing the rice until it's heated through.
- Once the rice is hot, add the remaining ingredients (including the eggs), Continue to cook over medium heat, mixing continuously for 2- 3 minutes.
- Taste and season with pepper and any additional soy sauce that may be needed.

MEDITERRANEAN CAULIFLOWER RICE

INGREDIENTS

- 1 medium-to-large head cauliflower or 16 ounces store-bought cauliflower rice
- ½ cup sliced almonds
- 2 tablespoons extra-virgin olive oil
- 2 cloves garlic, pressed or minced
- Pinch of red pepper flakes (omit if sensitive to spice)
- ¼ teaspoon fine sea salt
- ½ cup chopped flat-leaf parsley
- 1 tablespoon lemon juice
- Freshly ground black pepper, to taste

INSTRUCTIONS

- If you're working with a head of cauliflower, cut it into medium chunks and discard the core. Working in batches, pulse the chunks in a food processor with the S-blade until they're broken into tiny pieces, just bigger than couscous.

- Wrap the cauliflower rice in a clean tea towels or paper towels, twist, and squeeze as much water as possible from the rice—you might be surprised by how much water you can wring out.

- Toast the almonds in a large skillet over medium heat, stirring frequently (careful, or they'll burn), until they're fragrant and starting to turn golden on the edges, about 3 to 5 minutes. Transfer the toasted almonds to a bowl to cool.

- Return the skillet to the heat and add the olive oil and garlic. Cook while stirring until the garlic is fragrant, about 10 to 20 seconds. Add the cauliflower rice, red pepper flakes and salt, and stir to combine. Cook, stirring just every minute

- or so, until the cauliflower rice is hot and turning golden in places, about 6 to 10 minutes.

- Remove the skillet from the heat. Stir in the toasted almonds, parsley and lemon juice. Season to taste with salt and pepper, and serve warm.

BROWN RICE STIR-FRY WITH VEGETABLES

Ingredients

- 1/2 cup uncooked brown rice (100 g)
- 1 cup chopped red cabbage (80 g)
- 1/2 head of broccoli, chopped
- 1/2 chopped red bell pepper
- 1/2 chopped zucchini
- 2 tbsp extra virgin olive oil
- 4 cloves of garlic, minced
- 1 handful fresh parsley, finely chopped

- 1/8 tsp cayenne powder

- 2 tbsp tamari or soy sauce

- Sesame seeds for garnish (optional)

Instructions

- Cook the brown rice according to package directions.

- Place some water in a wok or frying pan and bring it to a boil. Then add the veggies (they must be covered by the water) and cook for 1 to 2 minutes over high-heat. Drain the veggies and set aside.

- Heat the oil in the wok and add the garlic, cayenne powder and parsley. Cook over high-heat for about 1 minute, stirring occasionally.

- Add the vegetables, rice and tamari. Cook for about 1 to 2 minutes more.

- Add some sesame seeds for garnish (optional).

- Store the brown rice stir-fry in a sealed container in the fridge for up to 5 days.
- Notes
- Feel free to use other grains, veggies, spices or any other non-refined oil.
- To make an oil-free recipe, just cook the garlic, cayenne powder and parsley in some water or oil-free broth. You could also omit step number 3, use some garlic powder and cook it with the cayenne powder, parsley, veggies and rice for a few minutes.
- If you don't like spicy food, omit the cayenne powder or add less.

FIESTA RICE RECIPE

Ingredients

- 2 tablespoons butter
- 1 yellow onion , diced

- 1 small red pepper , diced
- 2 to 3 garlic cloves , minced
- 1-1/4 cups uncooked long grain rice
- 1 can (10 ounces) diced tomatoes with green chilies
- 1 can (15 ounces) reduced sodium black beans, rinsed
- 1 can (15 ounces) sweet corn kernels, rinsed
- 1 teaspoon ground cumin, OR to taste
- 1/4 teaspoon salt
- 1/8 teaspoon fresh ground pepper
- 2 cups organic low sodium vegetable broth
- chopped cilantro
- 1 tablespoon fresh lime juice

Instructions

- Melt butter in a large nonstick skillet over medium-high heat.

- Add onions and red peppers; cook for 3 minutes.
- Stir in garlic and continue to cook for 30 seconds.
- Add rice and cook, stirring often, for 2 minutes.
- Stir in diced tomatoes with green chilies, black beans, and corn.
- Season with cumin, salt and fresh ground pepper.
- Stir in vegetable broth and bring to a boil.
- *Cover, reduce heat to low, and cook for 15 to 20 minutes, or until liquid is absorbed.
- Remove cover, fluff with fork and stir in cilantro and lime juice.
- Serve.

CHICKEN BROWN RICE MEAL PREP

Ingredients

- 4 chicken breasts
- 1 tbsp unsalted butter
- 21/2 tsp olive oil
- 2 medium broccoli (cut into small florets)
- 1 cup zucchini (round slices)
- 1 cup baby tomatoes (halved)
- 3 lemons (freshly squeezed juice)
- 1 tbsp pepper powder
- 1 tbsp Italian seasoning
- 10 cloves garlic (minced)
- 2 cups brown rice (cooked)
- 1/2 cup cilantro
- 4 lemon(or lime) wedges
- salt to taste

Instructions

- Cook brown rice until nice and fluffy. Check out how to cook rice in instant pot. Once cooked keep aside to cool.

- Add juice of 1 lemon, salt to taste and ½ cup chopped cilantro into rice. Give it a gentle mix.

- Marinate chicken breasts with lemon juice, salt to taste, pepper powder, Italian seasoning. Mix well and let it sit in fridge until use.

- In a pan heat an teaspoon oil. Stir fry broccoli florets seasoned with little salt for about 2 minutes or so. Remove from pan on to a plate.

- Stir fry zucchini slices in the same pan for a minute or so. Remove zucchini on to a plate.

- Throw in the baby tomatoes and let it blister in the pan, takes about a minute depending on the heat of the pan.

- Add the butter and remaining olive oil.
  Arrange marinated chicken breasts in the
  pan. Add minced garlic on sides of the
  pan. Cook chicken on both sides until
  seared well. Remove from pan once
  cooked, let it cool. Slice.

- Portion chicken, rice, vegetables between
  4 storage containers. Top it with some
  more cilantro leaves.

- Serve immediately, or cover tightly with
  lids and refrigerate for up to 4 days.

5-INGREDIENT VEGETABLE FRIED BROWN RICE

INGREDIENTS

- 1 teaspoon coconut oil (or other high heat
  cooking oil)

- 2 eggs, lightly whisked

- 1 cup frozen mixed vegetables

- 2 cups cooked brown rice
- 1/4 – 1/3 cup low sodium soy sauce

INSTRUCTIONS

- Heat oil in a large wok over medium high heat.
- Add frozen mixed vegetables and cook for 2 minutes, stirring frequently. Add brown rice and soy sauce to vegetables and cook for up to 5 minutes or until all is heated through.
- Make a well in the center of the vegetables and rice and add whisked eggs to wok. Let cook and set for a minute. Break up eggs with your spatula or spoon into small pieces. Stir into fried rice.
- Season well with coarse salt, fresh ground pepper and additional soy sauce to taste. Serve with red chili sauce or sriracha.

GARLIC CHICKEN FRIED BROWN RICE

Ingredient

- 2 tablespoons vegetable oil, divided
- 8 ounces skinless, boneless chicken breast, cut into strips
- ½ red bell pepper, chopped
- ½ cup green onion, chopped
- 4 cloves garlic, minced
- 3 cups cooked brown rice
- 2 tablespoons light soy sauce
- 1 tablespoon rice vinegar
- 1 cup frozen peas, thawed

Directions

- Heat 1 tablespoon of vegetable oil in a large skillet set over medium heat. Add the chicken, bell pepper, green onion and garlic. Cook and stir until the chicken is cooked through, about 5 minutes.

Remove the chicken to a plate and keep warm.

- Heat the remaining tablespoon of oil in the same skillet over medium-high heat. Add the rice; cook and stir to heat through. Stir in the soy sauce, rice vinegar and peas, and continue to cook for 1 minute. Return the chicken mixture to the skillet and stir to blend with the rice and heat through before serving.

SHEET PAN BALSAMIC BASIL CHICKEN CAULIFLOWER RICE BOWL

INGREDIENTS

- 2 cups riced cauliflower
- 3 cups broccoli florets
- 1 medium red onion, sliced
- 4 chicken breasts, diced, boneless, skinless

- 1/4 cup balsamic vinegar

- salt & pepper to taste

- 3 tbsp olive oil, extra virgin

- 1 tbsp minced garlic

- 1/8 cup fresh basil, chopped

INSTRUCTIONS

- Preheat oven to 400 degrees.

- Spread diced chicken in a single layer on one side of your baking sheet.

- Add broccoli florets to baking sheet in a single layer beside your chicken. Cut any large florets in half or thirds.

- Spread sliced red onion in a single layer on baking sheet beside the broccoli.

- Add cauliflower rice to baking sheet beside the onion. (If you're ricing your own cauliflower just add florets to a high powered blender and blend until cauliflower has a rice or pearl-like consistency.)

- Drizzle 1/4 cup balsamic vinegar over the chicken and broccoli.
- Add minced garlic to your chicken.
- Add salt, pepper, and olive oil to everything on the baking sheet.
- Bake for 15 minutes.
- Remove from the oven and separate the chicken if it's sticking together. Place back in the oven and bake for 5 additional minutes or until chicken is cooked through..
- Layer your cauliflower rice, red onions, broccoli, and chicken in bowls. Add a little more balsamic vinegar if you prefer a stronger taste (I always do) or more salt and pepper. Top with basil.

NOTES

- Dicing the chicken breasts allows them to cook through quickly and absorb more balsamic vinegar. Plus, it means when everything is done baking all you'll have to do is build your veggie bowls!

- Many people do not use olive oil when preparing this sheet pan meal to keep it extra light. You can omit if you prefer.

TERIYAKI TURKEY RICE BOWL

INGREDIENTS

Teriyaki Sauce

- 1/2 cup Low Sodium Soy Sauce

- 1/4 cup water

- 2 tablespoons Red Wine Vinegar

- 2 tablespoons brown sugar or less as desired

- 2 tablespoons granulated sugar or less as desired

- 2 teaspoons minced garlic

- 1 teaspoon ground ginger

- 1 tablespoon cornstarch

- 2 tablespoons warm water

Ground Turkey

- 1 tablespoon vegetable oil

- 1/2 cup diced onion

- 2 tablespoons minced garlic

- 1 pound Ground Turkey

- 1 cup finely chopped broccoli

- 2 large carrots peeled and grated

- 2 green onions diced, for garnish

INSTRUCTIONS

- Mix soy sauce, 1/4 cup water, red wine vinegar, sugars, garlic and ginger in a small saucepan over medium heat. Stir with a whisk until sugar is dissolved.

- In a small bowl, whisk together 2 tablespoons warm water and cornstarch until cornstarch is completely dissolved.

- Heat sauce over medium high heat. Slowly whisk in cornstarch mixture and simmer until thickened. Remove from heat and set aside.

- Heat vegetable oil in a large skillet over medium-high heat. Add diced onions and cook until soft.

- Crumble ground turkey and garlic into the pan and cook until turkey is about half cooked. Add grated carrots and chopped broccoli and continue to cook until turkey is no longer pink.

- Pour teriyaki sauce over cooked turkey and vegetable mixture and stir. Simmer for about five minutes to combine the flavors.

- Spoon meat over rice or noodles. Garnish with green onions and serve immediately.

EASY BETTER-THAN-TAKEOUT CHICKEN FRIED RICE

INGREDIENTS:

- 2 tablespoons sesame oil
- 2 tablespoons canola or vegetable oil
- 3/4 to 1 pound boneless skinless chicken breasts, diced into 1/2-inch pieces
- 1 1/2 cups frozen peas and diced carrots blend
- 3 green onions, trimmed and sliced into thin rounds
- 2 to 3 garlic cloves, finely minced
- 3 large eggs, lightly beaten
- 4 cups cooked rice (I use white, long-grain or brown may be substituted. To save

time use two 8.8-ounce pouches cooked and ready-to-serve rice)

- 3 to 4 tablespoons low-sodium soy sauce
- salt and pepper, optional and to taste

DIRECTIONS:

- To a large non-stick skillet or wok, add the oils, chicken, and cook over medium-high heat for about 3 to 5 minutes, flipping intermittently so all sides cook evenly. Cooking time will vary based on thickness of chicken breasts and sizes of pieces. Remove chicken with a slotted spoon (allow oils and cooking juices from chicken to remain in skillet) and place chicken on a plate; set aside.
- Add the peas, carrots, green onions, and cook for about 2 minutes, or until vegetables begin to soften, stir intermittently.

- Add the garlic and cook for 1 minute, stir
  intermittently.

- Push vegetables to one side of the skillet,
  add the eggs to the other side, and cook
  to scramble, stirring as necessary.

- Add the chicken, rice, evenly drizzle with
  soy sauce, optional salt and pepper, and
  stir to combine. Cook for about 2 minutes,
  or until chicken is reheated through.
  Recipe is best warm and fresh but will
  keep airtight in the fridge for up to 5 days
  or in the freezer for up to 4 months.
  Reheat gently as desired.

RESTAURANT STYLE MEXICAN RICE

Ingredients

- 3 tablespoons vegetable oil

- 1 cup long grain rice uncooked

- 1 teaspoon minced garlic

- 1/2 teaspoon kosher salt

- 1/2 teaspoon cumin

- 1/2 cup tomato sauce

- 14 ounces chicken broth

- 3 tablespoons fresh cilantro finely chopped

Instructions

- Heat oil in a large sauce pan over medium heat.

- Add the rice and gently stir until rice begins to lightly brown.

- Add the garlic, salt, and cumin and stir the rice til it looks golden.

- Add the tomato sauce and chicken broth and turn the heat up to medium high.

- Bring the mix to a boil then turn the heat to low and cover the pan with a lid.

- Simmer for 20 to 25 minutes.

- Remove from heat and fluff with a fork, then stir in chopped cilantro.

ONE-POT CHICKEN AND RICE

Ingredients

- 4 - 6 Tablespoons butter or vegan butter, divided
- 1 heaping cup chopped carrots (from 1 cup baby carrots or 2 large carrots)
- homemade seasoned salt and pepper
- 2 scant cups long grain white rice
- 1 Tablespoon dried minced onion
- 1 teaspoon dried minced garlic
- 2 Tablespoons dried parsley flakes
- 8 cups gluten free chicken stock
- 2 small chicken breasts (14oz), cut into bite-sized pieces

Directions

- Melt 2 Tablespoons butter in a soup pot over medium heat. Add carrots, season with seasoned salt and pepper, then place a lid on top and cook until carrots are tender, 5-6 minutes, stirring occasionally.

- Add rice, dried onions and dried garlic then stir to coat in butter and saute for 1 minute. Add dried parsley and chicken stock then turn heat up to high to bring to a boil, stirring occasionally to ensure rice doesn't stick to the bottom of the pot as it comes to a boil.

- Turn heat down to medium-low then simmer for 10 minutes, stirring occasionally. Season chicken with seasoned salt and pepper then add to the pot, turn heat up slightly to bring back up to a bubble, then turn back down to medium-low and continue to simmer until chicken is cooked through and rice is al dente, 12-15 more minutes, stirring occasionally and more frequently near the end.

- Place a lid on top of the pot then remove from heat and let sit for 5 minutes. Stir in remaining 2 - 4 Tablespoons butter (however much you like!) then season with additional seasoned salt and pepper if necessary. Scoop into bowls then serve. Note: dish will thicken as it cools.

CAJUN SHRIMP AND RICE SKILLET

Ingredients

- 1⅓ cups uncooked long grain white rice
- 2⅔ cup chicken broth
- 1 pound large or jumbo shrimp, peeled and de-veined
- 4 tablespoons butter, melted divided
- 1 teaspoon minced garlic

- cajun seasoning see below

- cajun seasoning

- 1½ teaspoons paprika

- 1 teaspoon salt

- 1 teaspoon garlic powder

- ½teaspoon cracked black pepper

- ½ teaspoon onion powder

- ½ teaspoon dried oregano may sub an Italian herb blend or Herbs de Provence

- ½ teaspoon cayenne pepper

- ¼ teaspoon crushed red pepper flakes

INSTRUCTIONS

- Whisk together all of the ingredients for the cajun seasoning. Melt 2 tablespoons butter in a large skillet over medium heat. Stir in garlic, half of the cajun seasoning, and the rice.

- Stir in chicken broth, bring to a boil,
  reduce to a simmer and cover. Cook for
  15 minutes, stirring 1-2 times throughout.

- While rice is cooking, prepare the shrimp
  by stirring together remaining 2 table
  spoons melted butter and remaining
  cajun seasoning. Pour over shrimp and
  toss to coat.

- Stir shrimp into the rice, cover and cook 3-
  5 minutes longer until shrimp is pink and
  opaque. Garnish with chopped parsley if
  desired and serve.

NOTES

- For browned shrimp, you can saute the
  shrimp in the pan at the start of the
  recipe, transfer to a plate and cover to
  keep warm until the end, then stir into
  rice and serve.

PERFECT JASMINE RICE

INGREDIENTS

- 2-¾ cups water, plus more if necessary

- 1-½ cups jasmine rice

- ¾ teaspoon salt

INSTRUCTIONS

- Bring the water to a boil in a medium saucepan.

- Stir in the rice and the salt; cover and reduce the heat to low.

- Simmer for 15 minutes until all of the water is absorbed.

- Taste the rice; if it is still too firm, add a few more tablespoons of water.

- Cover the pan and let the rice absorb the water off of the heat.

SAFFRON RICE

- Ingredients

- ¼ tsp good quality saffron threads

- ¼ cup hot water

- 2 tbsp extra virgin olive oil

- ¾ cup minced yellow onion

- 2 cups white basmati rice

- 3 cups chicken stock or vegetable stock (if using vegetable stock, choose a golden colored stock such as "no chicken" broth)

- ¾ tsp salt (if using a low sodium stock, adjust salt to 1 tsp)

Instructions

- Note: it's important to use a good quality saffron for this recipe. There are several types of "faux safrron" on the market which are inexpensive, but flavorless. True saffron is very pricey, but you only need a little to add a lot of flavor.

- Take one half of the 1/4 tsp saffron threads and put them in a spice mortar. Grind the spice with a pestle to a powdery consistency.
- Ground saffron threads in a mortar and pestle.
- Add a second pinch of saffron threads to the mortar. Do not crush these threads.
- Pour 1/4 cup of hot water into the mortar. Let the saffron soak for 5 minutes. This will open up the flavor of the spice.
- Warm water added to saffron in a mortar.
- Meanwhile, sort your basmati rice and rinse in a colander. Drain.
- In a large heavy pot, heat extra virgin olive oil over medium. Add the minced onion to the pot and sauté for about 10 minutes, stirring very frequently, until the onion is very soft and begins to caramelize.
- Diced onion in a saucepan.

- Add rinsed rice to the pot and sauté for one minute longer, mixing the rice together with the cooked onion.

- White basmati rice in a saucepan.

- Pour the yellow saffron liquid evenly across the top of the rice.

- Saffron water added to cooked rice in a saucepan.

- Add chicken or vegetable stock and salt to the pot. Bring to a boil, stir. Bring back to a boil for 30 seconds.

- Boiling rice in a saucepan.

- Cover the pot and reduce heat to low. Let the rice cook for 20 minutes. Turn off the heat, but keep pot covered, and continue to let the rice sit and steam in the covered pot for 10 minutes longer.

- Cooked saffron rice in a saucepan.

- Fluff the rice with a fork before serving, stirring well to break up the rice and incorporate the cooked onion.

CHICKEN BURRITO SKILLET

INGREDIENTS

- 2 tablespoons canola oil
- 1 pound boneless skinless chicken breasts, cut into bite-size pieces
- 1/2 cup chopped yellow onion
- 2 tablespoons taco seasoning mix (from 1.25-oz pkg)
- 1 can (15 oz each) Rosarita Premium Whole Black Beans, drained, rinsed
- 1 can (10 oz each) Ro Tel Original Diced Tomatoes & Green Chilies, undrained
- 1 cup water
- 1-1/4 cups instant brown rice, uncooked

- 1 cup shredded Cheddar and Monterey Jack cheese blend
- Chopped cilantro, optional

DIRECTIONS

- Heat oil in large skillet over medium-high heat. Add chicken and cook 3 minutes, stirring occasionally. Add onion and taco seasoning; cook 2 minutes more. Stir in black beans, undrained tomatoes and water; bring to a boil.
- Stir in rice. Cover, reduce heat and simmer 7 to 10 minutes or until rice is tender. Stir in 1/2 cup cheese. Sprinkle top with remaining cheese and cilantro, if desired.

SPANISH RICE RECIPE

Ingredients

- 2 cups long grain rice
- 1/8 cup oil
- 8 oz tomato sauce
- 6 stems cilantro (optional)
- 1 tsp salt
- 1 tsp minced garlic
- 4 cups water
- 1 cube chicken flavored bouillon
- dash cumin
- dash garlic pepper

Instructions

- Heat oil in large frying pan on medium heat.
- Add rice and cook until golden brown.
- Add 1 chicken flavored bouillon cube to 4 cups water and microwave for 3 minutes.
- When rice is brown, add water, tomato sauce, salt, garlic, cumin and garlic pepper to pan.

- Stir and cover pan. Let simmer for 30-40 minutes or until all is cooked and there is no liquid left. Fluff before serving and ENJOY.

ONE-POT FRENCH ONION SOUP RICE SKILLET

Ingredients

- 1 lb ground beef
- 1 small yellow onion, diced
- 1 cup uncooked regular long-grain white rice
- 2½ cups Progresso beef-flavored broth (from 32-oz carton)
- 1 package (1 oz) onion soup mix
- ½ cup grated Gruyère cheese

Directions

- Heat 12-inch skillet over medium heat; add beef and onion. Cook until beef is no longer pink, crumbling beef as it cooks; drain.

- Stir in rice, broth, and onion soup mix. Heat to boiling; reduce heat to simmering. Cover and cook about 15 minutes, stirring halfway through, until rice is tender.

- Remove from heat; stir in cheese. Cover; let stand about 2 minutes or until melted.

MUSHROOM RISOTTO WITH PEAS

INGREDIENTS

- 6 to 7 cups chicken, vegetable or garlic broth or stock, as needed

- Salt and freshly ground pepper

- 2 tablespoons extra-virgin olive oil

- ½ cup finely chopped onion, or 2 shallots, minced

- ¾ to 1 pound wild mushrooms, cleaned if necessary and torn or sliced into smaller pieces if thick (small wild mushrooms should be left whole, mushrooms like maitake can just be separated into small pieces)
- 2 garlic cloves, minced
- 2 teaspoons fresh thyme leaves or chopped sage
- 1 ½ cups arborio or carnaroli rice
- ½ cup dry white wine, such as pinot grigio or sauvignon blanc
- 1 cup frozen peas, thawed (optional)
- 2 tablespoons chopped fresh parsley
- ½ cup grated Parmesan cheese, or a mixture of Parmesan and Pecorino Romano

Direction

- Bring stock or broth to a simmer in a saucepan, with a ladle nearby. Make sure stock is well seasoned, and keep it simmering on the stove.

- Heat oil in a wide, heavy nonstick skillet or saucepan over medium heat. Add onions or shallots and cook gently until just tender, 3 to 5 minutes.

- Turn up heat and add mushrooms. Cook, stirring, until they begin to sweat, about 3 minutes, then add garlic and thyme or sage. Cook, stirring, until fragrant, about 30 seconds. Season mushrooms with salt and pepper and continue to cook over medium heat until they are soft. Taste and adjust seasoning.

- Add rice and stir until grains begin to crackle. Add wine and cook, stirring, until wine is no longer visible in pan. Stir in enough simmering stock to just cover the rice. The stock should bubble slowly. Cook, stirring often and vigorously, until stock is just about absorbed. Add another ladleful or two of stock and continue cooking, not too fast and not too slowly, stirring often and adding more stock when rice is almost dry, for 15 minutes.

- Add peas, if using, and continue adding stock and stirring for another 10 minutes. Rice should be tender all the way through but still al dente. Taste now and adjust seasoning.
- Add another ladleful or two of stock to rice. Stir in parsley and Parmesan, and remove from heat. Season with black pepper and serve right away in wide soup bowls or on plates.

INGREDIENTS

- 1 teaspoon TABASCO brand Original Red Sauce
- 2 tablespoons vegetable oil
- ½ pound andouille or other smoked sausage, cut into 1/2-inch slices
- ½ cup sliced celery
- 1 small onion, chopped
- 1 small red or green bell pepper, chopped
- 1 clove garlic, minced
- 1¾ cups chicken broth
- 1 cup diced fresh or canned tomatoes
- 1 bay leaf
- ¼ teaspoon dried oregano leaves
- ¼ teaspoon dried thyme leaves
- ⅛ teaspoon ground allspice
- ¾ cup uncooked rice

- ½ pound shrimp, peeled, deveined and cut in half lengthwise

Direction

- Heat oil in a large heavy saucepan or Dutch oven over medium-high heat. Add sausage, celery, onion, bell pepper, and garlic.
- Cook 5 minutes or until vegetables are tender, stirring frequently.
- Stir in broth, tomatoes, bay leaf, TABASCO Sauce, oregano, thyme, and allspice. Bring to a boil, reduce heat, and simmer uncovered for 10 minutes, stirring occasionally. Stir in rice; cover and simmer 15 minutes. Add shrimp; cover and simmer 5 minutes longer or until rice is tender and shrimp turn pink. Let stand, covered, 10 minutes.
- Remove bay leaf before serving.

CONCLUSION

If you're interested in trying the rice diet method, talk with your doctor before making any drastic changes to your diet, especially if you have any medical conditions that affect your sodium levels.

Keep in mind that there's no such thing as a "diet" for weight loss. Instead, incorporate lifestyle changes that can help you maintain a healthy weight.